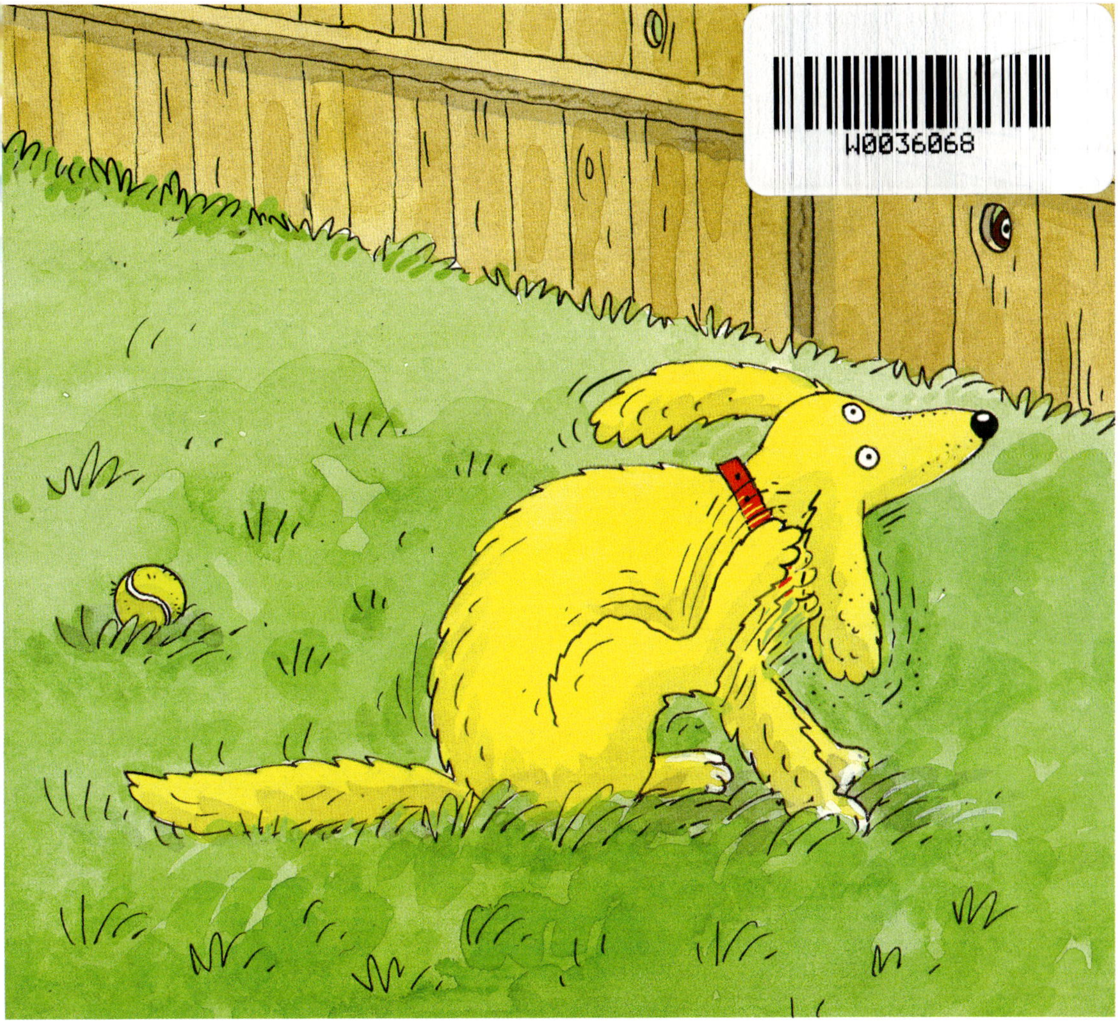

Floppy was in his back garden.

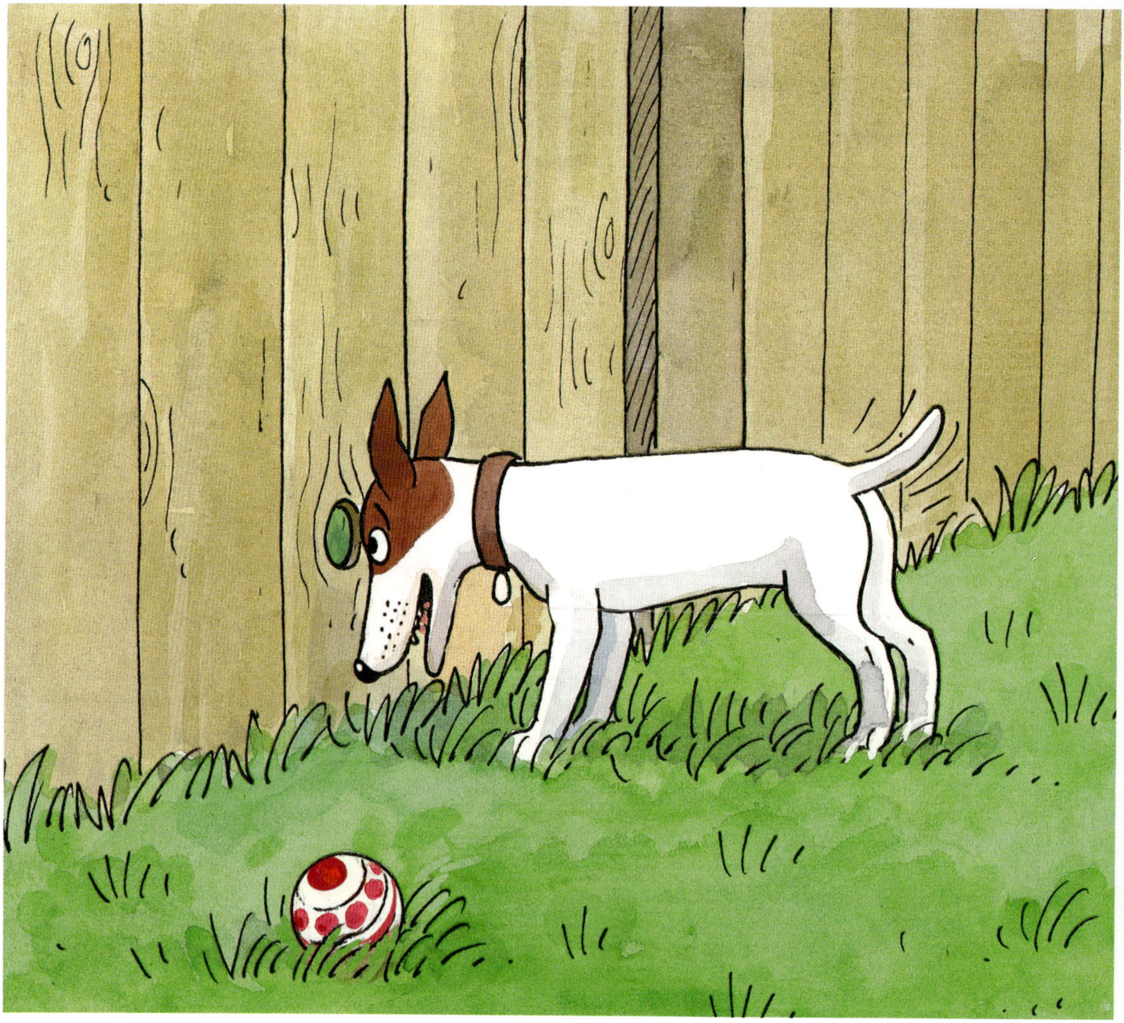

Button was in his
back garden.

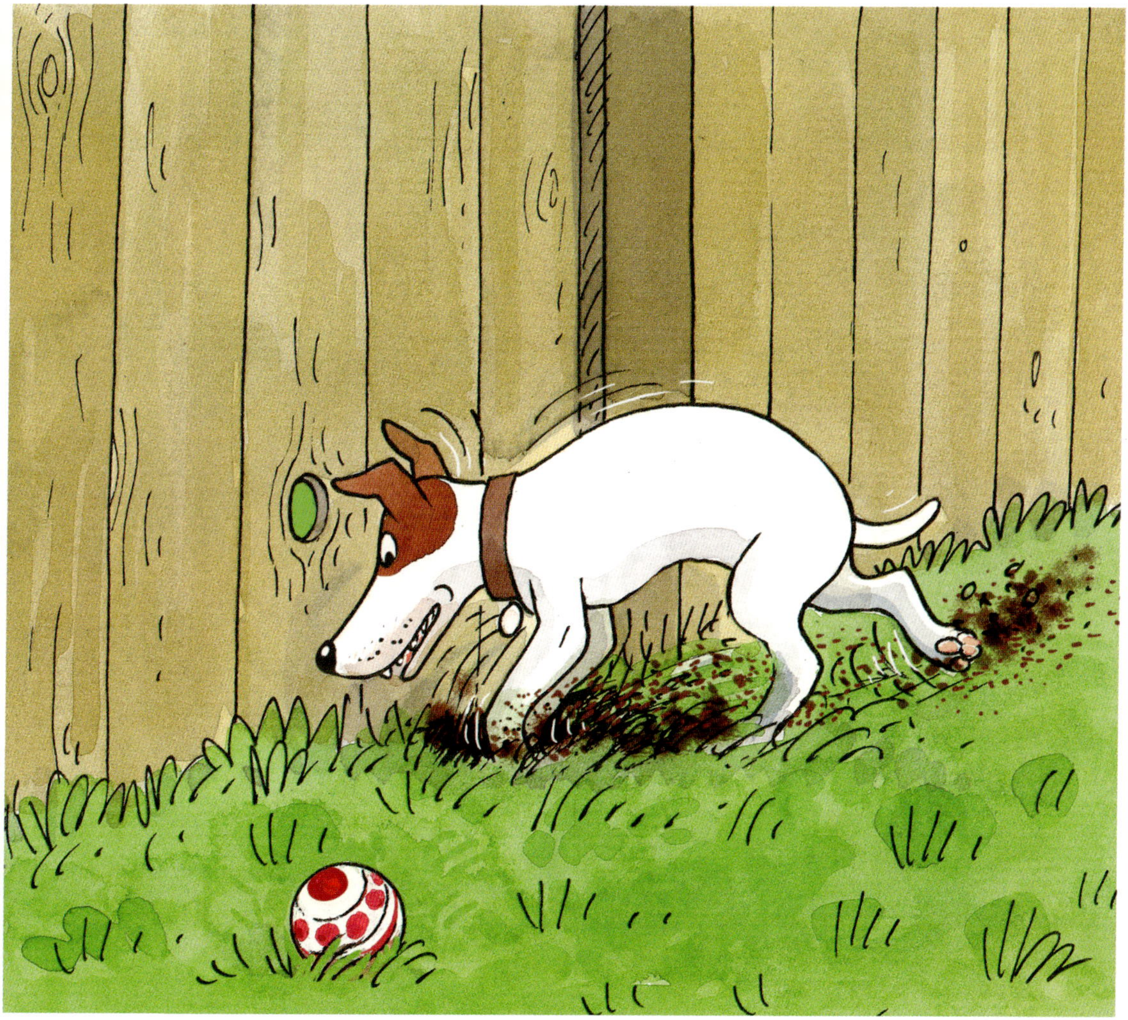

Button dug and dug . . .

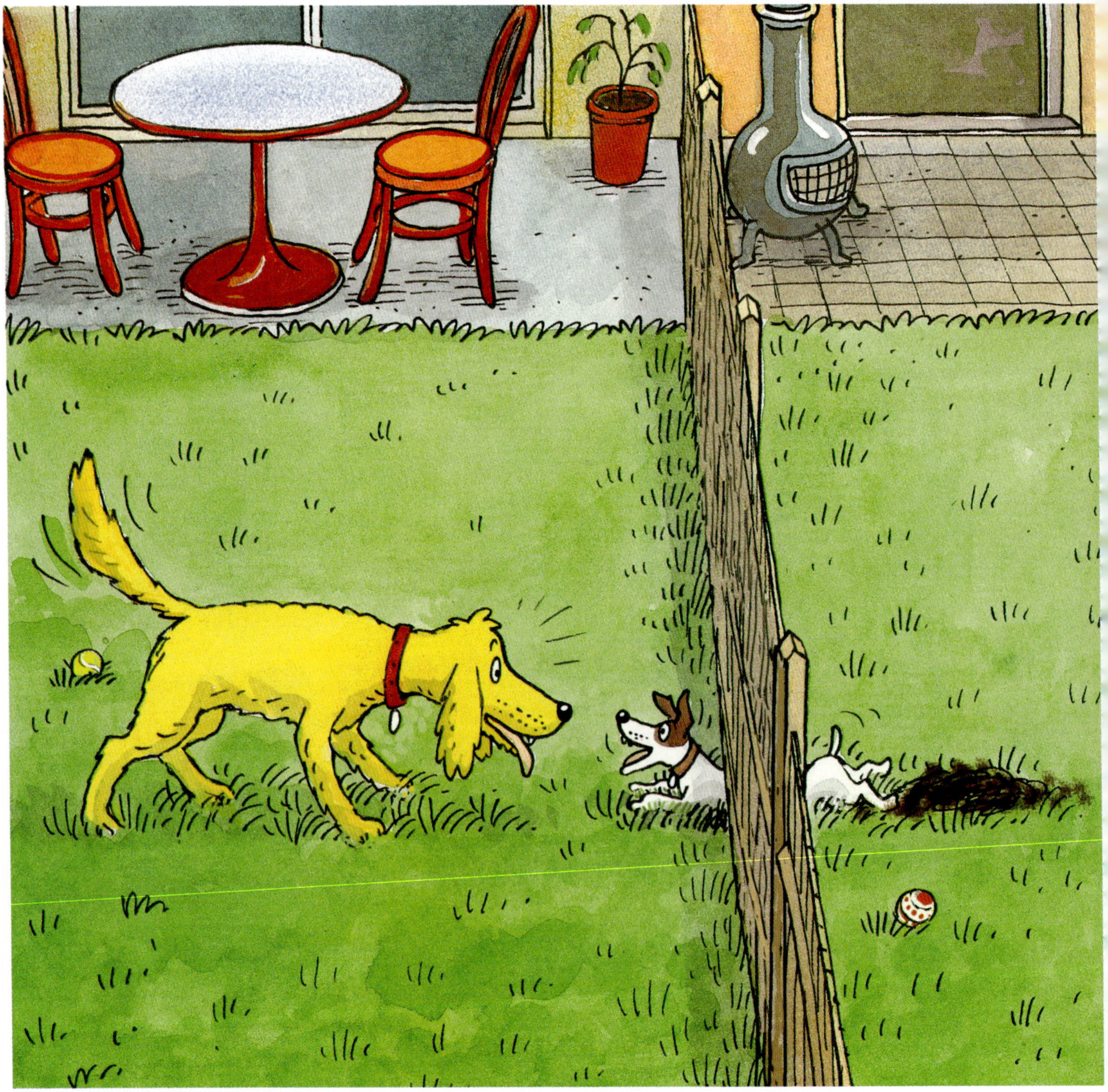

Button was stuck.

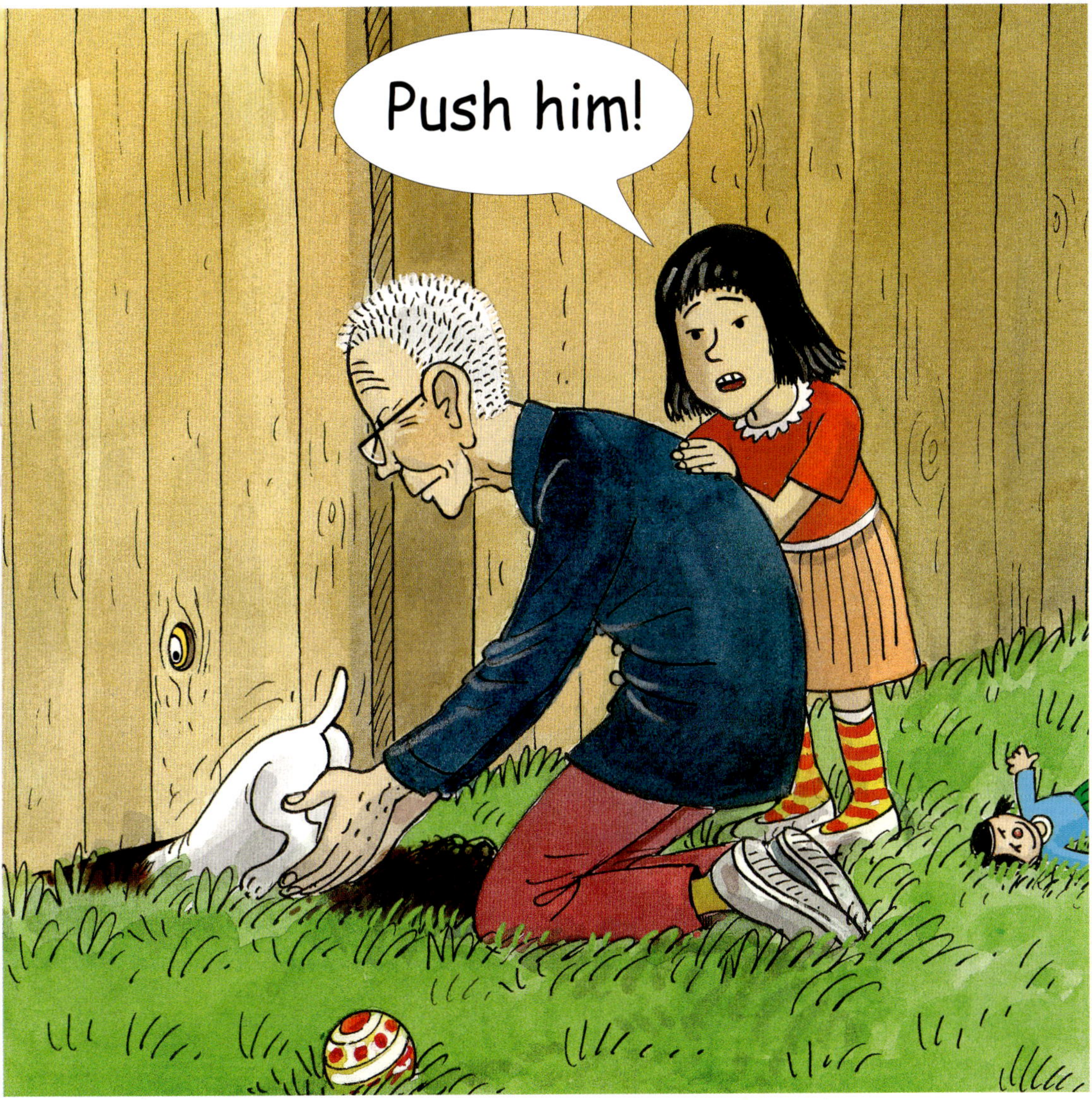

Button did not budge.

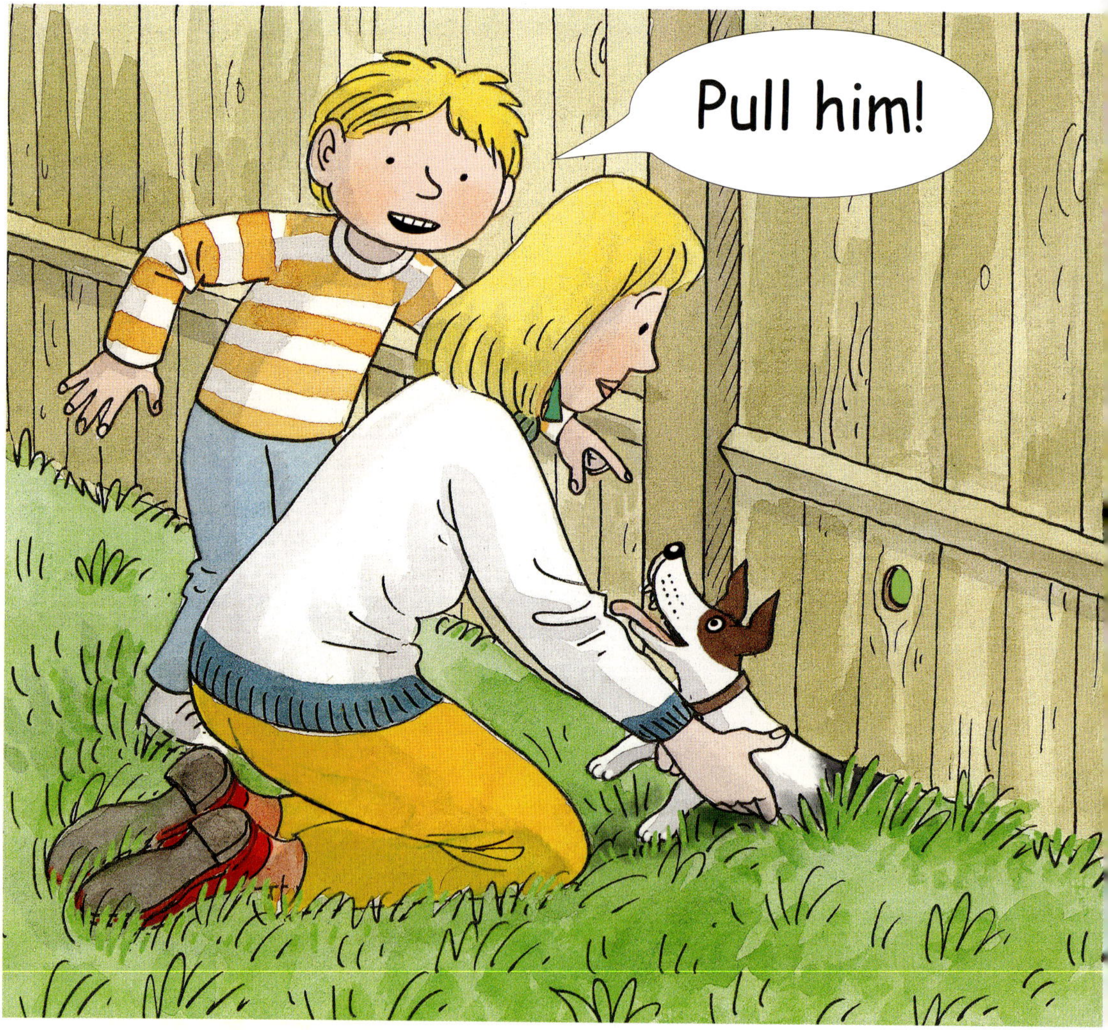

Button did not budge.

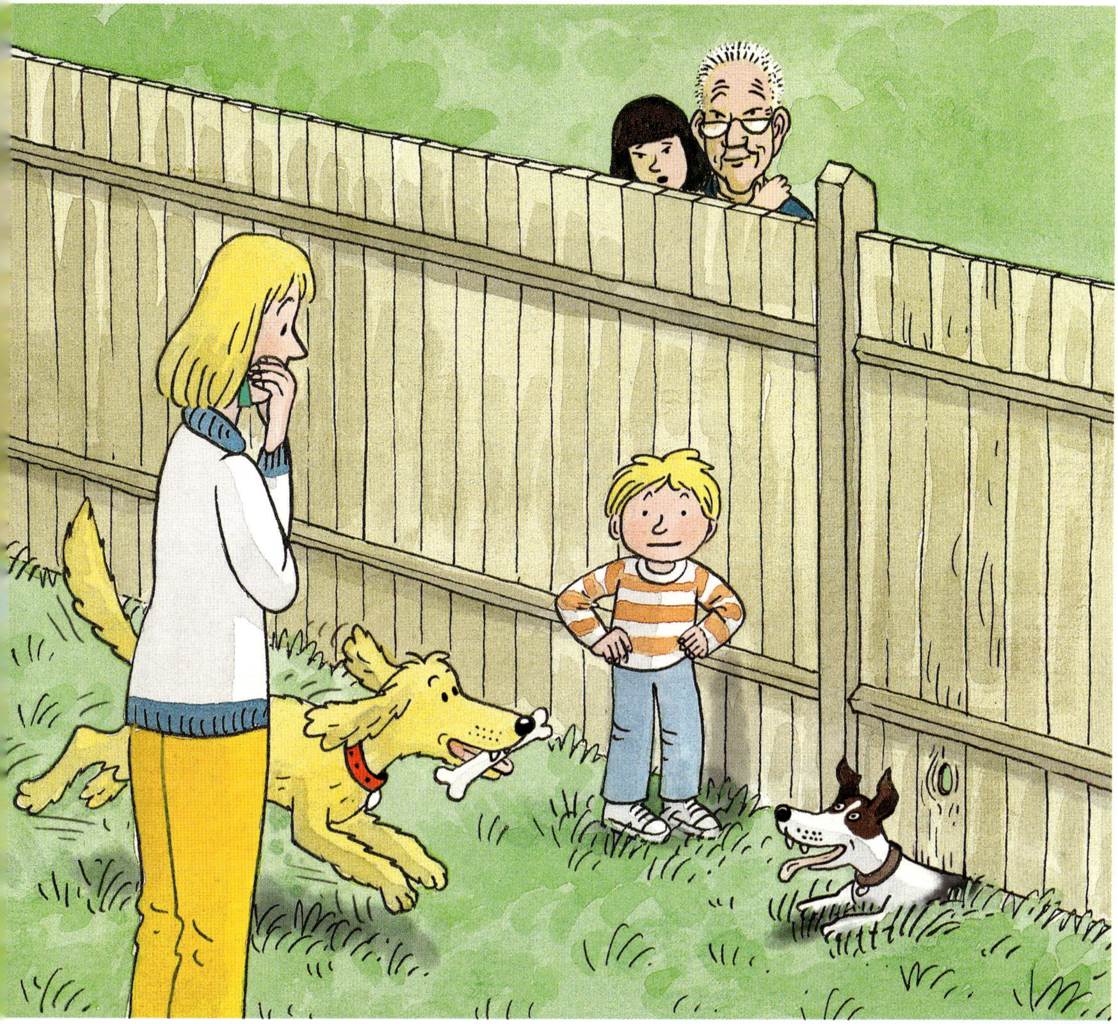

Floppy got a big bone
and . . .

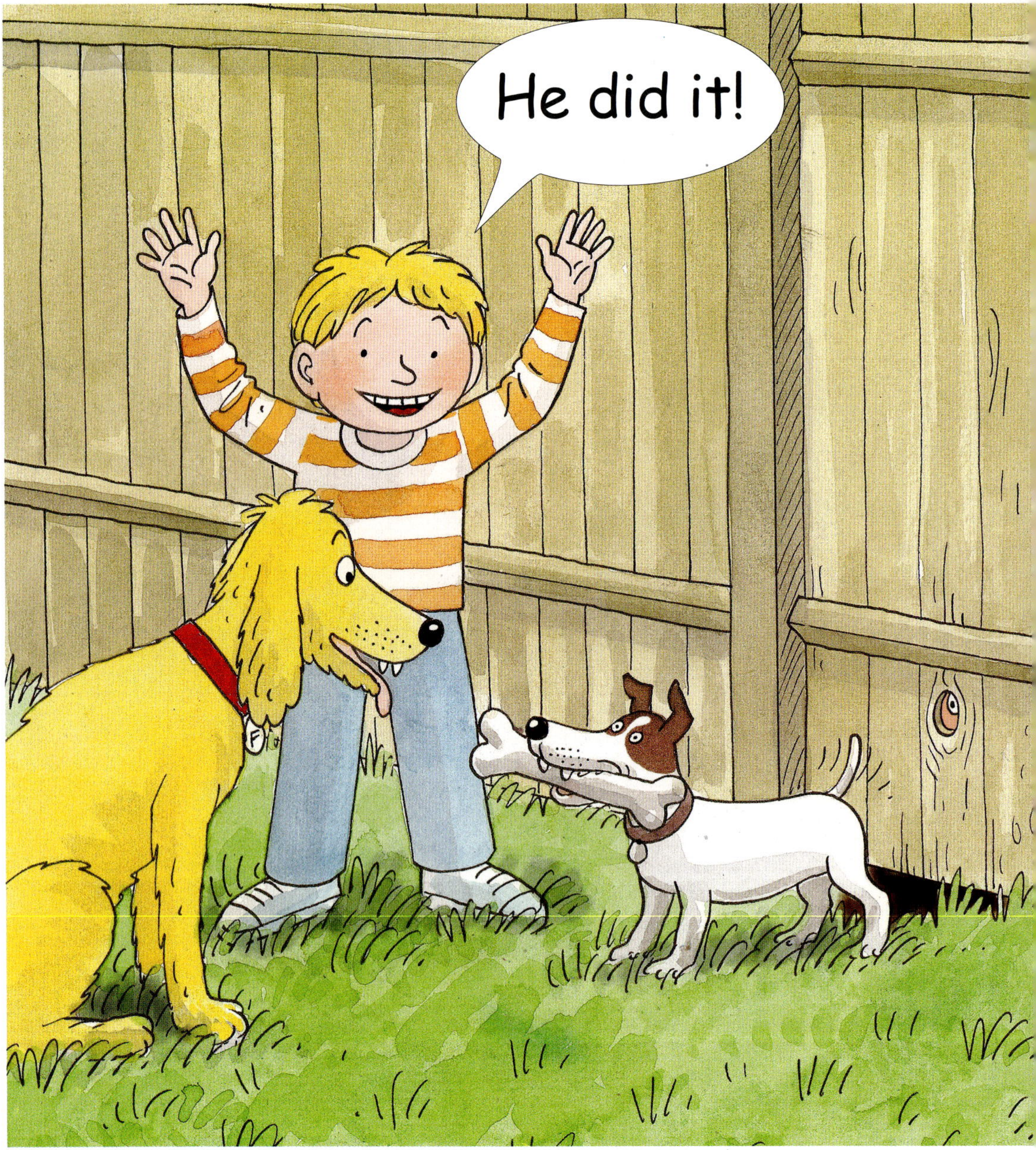
He did it!